Copyright, Legal Notice and Disclaimer:

This publication is protected under the US Copyright Act of 1976 and all other applicable international, federal, state and local laws, and all rights are reserved, including resale rights.

Please note that this publication is based on personal experience and anecdotal evidence. Although the author and publisher have made every reasonable attempt to achieve complete accuracy of the content in this Manual, they assume no responsibility for errors or omissions. You should use this information as you see fit, and at your own risk. Your particular situation may not be exactly suited to the examples illustrated in this book. You should adjust your use of the information and recommendations accordingly to your situation.

Any trademarks, service marks, product names or named features are assumed to be the property of their respective owners, and are used only for reference. There is no implied endorsement if we use one of these terms.

Nothing in this Manual is intended to replace common sense, legal, medical or other professional advice, and is meant to inform and entertain the reader. Always seek the advice of your medical physician, or other medical professional or qualified health care provider with any questions that you might have about a medical condition.

Never disregard advice from your medical professional or delay seeking medical advice because of anything you may have read in this manual.

Use of this book confirms that you accept all risks and responsibilities concerning your actions as a result of using any information provided in this book.

© 2011 Rachel A. Wheeler

All rights reserved.

ISBN-10: 0615677126
ISBN-13: 978-0-615-67712-5

The Kid Kash Program

Rachel A. Wheeler

Dedication

I want to dedicate this book and program to my beautiful children, Mikayla & Dylan who have made my life an everyday adventure. Through many trials and errors we have come to terms that we must each be responsible for our own actions, and that as a family we can achieve anything.

I also want to thank my wonderful husband for holding me when I cry, patting my back for being strong, and just loving me. Most of all for being a wonderful DAD!

CONTENTS

1	INTRODUCTION	11
2	Kid Kash Program	Pg#15
3	How to earn Money	Pg#21
4	Kid Kash Check Out List	Pg#25
5	Kid Kash Checkout Book	Pg#29
6	Kid Kash Dollar Bills	Pg#43
7	Kid Kash Double Money	Pg#83
8	Isolation Passes	Pg#93

Introduction

Let me first say that I am not perfect. I make mistakes every day. We all do. We are human. This is no different for children.

Let me give you a little history behind my program. I am a mother of two. I have a 12 year old daughter and a 9 year old son. Both are happy, healthy, vibrant kids. Each of them is uniquely different. My daughter, Mikayla loves horses, wants to barrel race, loves animals, is a nurturer, a writer, loves to cook, enjoys swimming, athletics, loves school and to laugh. She is an excellent student. Mostly A's with a few B's. I really have no discipline issues with her. She is very respectful and well mannered. However she tends to not "want" to do anything besides school. Everyday things such as brushing her teeth and getting dressed will sometimes take all day to accomplish on the weekends. While I understand that she works hard at school. There are responsibilities at home that she needs to attend to at home.

Here are her examples:

- Getting Dressed
- Brushing Teeth / Flossing Teeth
- Cleaning her room
- Helping with chores around the house
- Actually studying
- Making her bed

Now let's talk about my son Dylan. He is such a wonderful individual. He loves to paint, draw, and write stories too. He is a true inventor. Dylan will always find a way to create something or make something better. He likes karate, motorcycles, loves to cook, play with his friends, ride his skateboard, and of course swimming. Dylan was diagnosed ADHD/ADD at age 6. It was explained to me that he had a little of both from his pediatrician. We have tried several types of medicine that help with ADHD. Most did help with the focusing issues; however none helped with the tantrums. Then at age 7 ½ he was diagnosed with ODD. From there we were sent to a psychiatrist to confirm the diagnoses. Dylan has been seeing the psychiatrist for 2 years now for the ADHD and the ODD. He was placed on a med for the ODD in addition to his ADHD medicine. He also sees a therapist for cognitive behavioral therapy.

I have been in and out of the school since Dylan was in 1st grade, attending parent/teacher conferences. In Dylan's 2nd grade year I sent a registered letter to his school requesting an ARD to see if we could get Dylan help in the classroom. Instead of an "Official ARD" I received a meeting with Dylan's Counselor. There they explained to me that because Dylan was just ADHD that they do not have special education programs that cover ADHD, and that they could implement a 504 plan. If you are unsure of the 504 plan, it is for students that have ADHD/ ADD. It gives the student preferential seating near the teacher, extra time to finish work, basically it gives them more teacher help. The program is designed specifically for each child to help with their strengths and weaknesses. His second grade year went relatively smoothly other than homework time. So the psychiatrist implemented a medication to help with afternoon school work. Dylan's homework time would take us three hours to complete instead of the 20 to 30 minutes that it should have taken, even with medicine. There would be fits of frustration, screaming, crying, defiance, and the hiding of the homework. At one point we followed the advice of the Doctors and used a timer, and if he did not complete his homework within an hour he had to turn it in incomplete. We often found Dylan's homework shoved under his bed. He would tell us that he had no homework for the day. In fact there were occasions that he left it on the bus "accidently". We made it through that school year with four counselor/ teacher meetings for 504 adjustments and several parent/teacher conferences.

Dylan's 3rd grade year became a little harder. His new teacher was a little stricter. This year would mark a change for Dylan. The teacher and I worked closely to have Dylan tested on several levels through special education. We had him tested for dyslexia; he qualified in two of them but not three as required by the state. So he did not qualify. Then the teacher and I requested that he be tested on his IQ level to see if there was an underlying learning disability. This can only be done if they are not passing school, and with a lot of documentation over time substantiating the need. At the time he was reading on a 1st grade level, flipping his letters, spelling words on how they sound regardless of his spelling list, flipping his numbers for math, struggled in problem solving for Math. Dylan still writes like a second grader, even today. He is just too busy to bother making it neat.

He passed all the assessments. I wanted to cry, I knew that he needed help. But how? When we reached the end of the assessment reading she told me the tester did note that he could not focus on the task at hand, and that she frequently had to redirect him to complete the testing. So with the first Official ARD, Dylan's file would be forwarded to the school Psychologist for him to be tested for ADHD, and that if he was found to be ADHD through the school psychologist that they would implement programs to suit him for his education. She did in fact diagnose him as ADHD. After all this the school has now implemented programs to help him while he is in school.

Anyone that has a child with extreme ADHD and ODD understands fully what I am saying. Everyday tasks that were expected of him to complete were a challenge. I would have to ask him repeatedly to get out of bed for school, get dressed for school, brush his teeth, even to take his medicine. By the time Dylan would leave in the mornings I would be so stressed out. It isn't so much that he was just not doing what he was supposed to, it was he forgot. He gets so distracted that he often would forget his lunch or his coat.

Dylan is known for his tantrums. He often screams and cries so loudly that our neighbors could hear. This could be because I told him he could not have a giant bowl of ice cream for a snack. Anything could set this off. Quite often we would go to the grocery store and he would beg for a toy, and when he was told NO, it became quite the theatrical scene inside the store. There were times that I would pay for our groceries and get to the car and just start crying. As a family we do things such as picnic at the zoo, or go to dinner, swimming at the lake park, family movie night, and many other things families do. However once the tantrums became so extreme we hardly went anywhere. This scenario became very upsetting to me. I enjoy family time. It was not only my husband and I that paid for it, but it was also Mikayla. Everything became a challenge. I would often lie in bed at night and cry after a day out somewhere. It was no longer fun to vacation or to have a night out with the kids.

The therapists have suggested marbles to reward him, allowance, tickets, and many other tools. These did not work for him. We have tried grounding for the tantrums, no toys, no dessert, put him in time out (the naughty chair is what we call it), no privileges. There have been countless chore charts and calendars. Nothing worked. When he was grounded for a day, the next day he would do the exact same thing that he was originally grounded for. We would sit him down and explain to him that his behavior was unacceptable and that in order for him to not receive punishment he needed to stop the tantrums. To our dismay he would agree and then forget everything we had previously talked about.

Here are Dylan's Examples:

- Tantrums
- Crying
- Not doing his homework/ and school work
- Not cleaning his room
- Picking up after himself
- Table Manners (talking with food in his mouth)
- Not following directions at school
- Getting up for school in the mornings

We recently were relocated due to my husband's job. As a family we all agreed that a new change would be great for us. Dylan promised this year would be different. He promised since he was about to be ten that he would try a little harder. Two weeks after the relocation, Dylan was back to his old habits. Let me say both of my children have adjusted well to the move. They love the area that we relocated to. They love our new home and new life. They even enjoy their new schools. However, old habits die hard.

We have a lot of structure when it comes to home life. The kids go to bed at 8:00 pm on school nights, homework gets done when they get home, keep your rooms picked up, make your bed, brush your teeth, take a shower, put your clothes away, try your best at school, read at least 30 minutes, and help mom when she asks. They must ask to watch TV, to play on the computer, or even to go outside and play. We do not buy our children toys when we go to the store, we do not give in when they whine or complain to get something they want. We do not allow inappropriate language, clothing, or behavior. We do not buy the kids new clothes or shoes because they want them. They receive these twice a year. We do not permit name calling or hitting. We do not allow rude obnoxious behavior. They are not permitted to eat whenever and whatever they want. They have three meals and two snacks a day. We expect them to have manners at the dinner table and to pick up after themselves. We make them ride the bus to and from school. I can honestly say we are strict parents.

These are some of the things I believe all parents try to instill into their own children. But even these simple things can be a struggle. Our rules have not changed over the years, and yet to ask them to complete even the tiniest chore ended in whining or tantrums. Even with the occasional "I do not want to". I have found even to this day, teachers still think that his actions in school are a result of my actions as a parent. I have found that Dylan's teachers have to meet with me to understand him and us as parents. Blame is often easy to misplace.

I am unsure when my children began to feel so entitled to everything. They only receive gifts on holidays or their birthdays. As they have gotten older I have noticed more of the entitlement attitude. Although they received gifts on days such as their birthday, they expected to get what they asked for, and quite often they did receive what they wanted if it was within our budget or means.

Then one morning after the kids left for school, I sat and cried because the morning was very difficult. It was the same four times of asking nicely for Dylan to get out of bed. Then finally after the fifth time I had to remove his blankets. Then he became mad at me; from there it was whining over getting dressed, brushing his teeth, anything you can imagine was just too much to ask for. He was fighting with his sister because he wanted to. He would do anything to get a rise out of me or Mikayla because he was mad. Dylan is very good a manipulating people's emotions and playing off them to get what he wants. THAT IS IT! I have had enough I told him. I do this quite often, but like I explained before nothing gets through to him. I sat down after they got onto the bus that morning and devised a system.

For days I had been racking my brain and thinking of anything and everything that has not worked. I have learned that kids want immediate gratification, whatever that may be. That most children feel they deserve everything and that everything should be given to them. We will often tell our kids that nothing in life is free and we as parents have to work even to provide groceries and a place to live. We explain that their toys, cell phone, and even their lunches we pack cost money. We are often dismissed with "I know Mom". So here is my program, I call it Kid Kash. Developed by me and enhanced by my children.

The Kid Kash Program

Step 1 – The Mentality

There are two things to remember when starting or using my program.

1. Nothing in life is FREE
2. Everything your kids have cost you MONEY!

You cannot walk into a store and demand that they give you a can of coffee without paying for it. You cannot watch TV without paying for electricity, or drive them to their extracurricular activities without purchasing fuel, or surf the internet without paying for internet connection. Your cell phones cost you money. Showering, washing clothes, and even brushing your teeth cost you. If you do not pay for water then you cannot cook or clean. I am sure you get the idea. While every parent wants to give their children their hearts desires, you must remember that you as a parent pay for everything.

Step 2 – Program Layout

1. 200 KID KASH dollar bills
2. 50 KID KASH two dollar bills. These are DOUBLE MONEY.
3. A roll of tickets. These are TEACHER TOKENS. (Can be purchased at a party store)
4. 60 minute bell timer (Can be purchased at any local store)
5. Payout Chart Summary
6. Kid Kash Store Checkout Book (14 Pages)
7. Kid Kash Store Pricelist
8. (1) Plastic Jar with Label (Can use anything for this or purchase from the store)
9. Isolation Passes
10. Kid Kash Manual

Step 3 – Understanding the Program Rules

Rule # 1 – Everything in Mom/Dad's Store Cost Money

- This includes toys, snacks, juices, cokes, TV time, outside time, time with friends, and etc. Please refer to Mom/Dad's Store Pricelist. You may add or remove anything that is not applicable within your household. Remember when a toy, cell phone, radio is purchased it is for the day. Each toy is $1.00. Meaning each item = $1.00. An Example:

  o Baseball and Baseball glove = $2.00

Items that are purchased are for that DAY only, make sure that each child returns them nightly to the store. THEY ARE REQUIRED TO PAY FOR THE ITEM AND THEY MUST WRITE DOWN EACH ITEM THEY WOULD LIKE TO PURCHASE ON THE CHECKOUT BOOK BEFORE REMOVING THE ITEM FROM THE STORE.

DO NOT CHARGE FOR MEALS – BREAKFAST, LUNCH, AND DINNER…

Rule #2 – They get paid for basic items when they are completed. You must pay them immediately after completion. Please double check to ensure they are completed prior to paying them.

- Getting Dressed - $1.00
- Brushing Teeth - $1.00
- Flossing Teeth - $1.00
- Brush and Fix Hair - $1.00
- Showering - $1.00

Rule #3 – There are fees for behavior. When the behavior occurs you must charge them right then. DO NOT TELL THEM GIVE ME YOUR MONEY! Say "Whining cost $2.00", then hold out your hand and tell them to pay you. THEY MUST WRITE DOWN THE CHARGE ON THE CHECKOUT BOOK. This enables them to understand and remember why they were charged for the type of negative behavior. Remind them that after $10.00 worth of behavior fees they receive ISOLATION. Please see pages 10-11 for explanation on isolation.

Rule #4 – There are REMINDER FEES. REMINDER FEES ARE DOUBLE WHAT THE REMINDER WAS FOR. If you have to remind them to brush their teeth, you would charge double what you would have paid out. It is important to have a cutoff time in the evenings or in the mornings; such as 10: 00 am.

An Example:

- Brushing Teeth = You would payout $1.00, reminding fee $1.00 (Cost $2.00)

Rule #3 – Utilize the Payout Chart. This is a great way for them to earn extra money. It has basic chores and the amounts for each. It also lets them choose how much money they can make. You will be surprised what is completed on this Payout chart. If they ask how to make more money, refer them back to the Payout Chart and let them choose. Make them accountable for earning their money. The Payout Chart has items that can be completed unlimited times a day, twice a day, once a day, and once a week. This prevents them from taking five showers to earn five dollars.

Rule #4 – If you ask them to do something and they do not want to do it. Explain to them that they will get paid for taking out the trash, but if MOM has to do it they have to pay you to do it. (This rule should only be used when there are things that you ASK them to complete)

An Example:

- Trash – You would payout $1.00, if you complete it charge them $2.00

This encourages them to complete the task when asked the first time. Remember do not feel bad for charging them. Privileges are purchased. No Money = No Privileges

Rule #5 – DO NOT GIVE THEM ANYTHING FOR FREE. This is a bad habit to start. You will not be able to explain to them why one thing was free and not the other. Keep with the principles that **NOTHING IN LIFE IS FREE.**

- Privacy is a Privilege – Door Shut 1 HR = $1.00
- Sleeping past 9:00 am on weekends – 1 HR = $1.00

- Staying up past bedtime – 1 HR (Set limits – An example my kids bedtime on school days is 8:00 pm and 10:00 pm on weekends. They can only purchase until 9:00 pm on school days and Midnight on weekends)

Step 4 – Removing their items

Remove it ALL. **Everything except their bed, clothing items, and books.**

Examples:

- Toys
- Cell phone
- Radio
- Handheld Video Games
- TV
- Game Consoles
- IPOD
- Night lights
- Stuffed Animals

You should have your children help with this. Next place everything in a central location. I personally use my living room. It does not make for a pretty living room, but I can say my home is more peaceful.

There will be arguing and tantrums thrown over this, however just remind them they are responsible for earning the money to play with these things.

After a set amount of time that you determine, you can allow their things to return to their room. Once the program has been established, they can then be responsible to report what they are purchasing.

Step 5 – Utilizing the Tools

Once everything is removed, sit down with your children and explain to them the concept of the program.

1. Layout each item for them to see.
2. Begin with the basic information that they will have to pay to use anything in Mom/Dad's Store.
3. Next, explain the Payout Chart. Explain that this is how they can earn money and they are responsible for earning their own money. Put this in a central location so that is accessible for the kids.
4. Kid Kash Store is a daily checkout only. Items removed without prior payment and written on the checkout list is stealing and will cost $5.00
5. Items not returned prior to the end of the night is also stealing, they are responsible for returning items to the store.

6. Show them the KID KASH one dollar bills. **It is important to understand that the reason you use mostly one dollar bills is because to most kids a $5.00 dollar bill is one item, however the same $5.00 in one dollar bills is five items.**
7. Next show them the DOUBLE KID KASH two dollar bills. These are only to be used when you are away from home and they display good behavior. DO NOT give these out for normal money earned. This is a special treat to earn double money, and should be used as such. It is very important that they understand that they determine how much they make when you are out on a trip to the grocery store or out to dinner. The better the behavior the more money they can earn. The most I would recommend giving for this is a total of $6.00 or (3) Double Money Bills.
8. The use of the Timer – When utilizing the timer it is important for them to understand that they are in control and responsible for time purchased. Only use the timer in one hour intervals. Have them take it with them or place it in a place that they can hear it.
    a. An Example: Dylan wants to buy an hour to play with his friends outside. He fills out the checkout list and gives me the money to play. He then sets the timer and places it on the porch so he can hear it when his time is up. Once his time is up he will then come in and either buy another hour or he will stay inside. When he purchases the extra hour he then resets his timer for an hour and goes back out to play.
9. The Savings Jar – This program explained that you will need to find or purchase a savings jar. It is important that the kids keep track of their own money. If money is lost, DO NOT replace lost money. Explain this concept to them. When adults lose money it is not replaced.
10. **Teacher Tokens** are a great way to get the results you want within the classroom. A lot of teachers give out paper money or tickets. Each token is worth a $1.00 in Kid Kash. Staple a zip lock bag in your child's homework folder, with a sharpie write teacher tokens. When your child gets home ask them if there are any Teacher Tokens that they want to cash in. At the end of the six weeks or whenever they can cash them out at school, return the ones that they exchanged for Kid Kash.

    A note: I personally met with my son's teachers and explained the program, I asked that they give him tickets as soon as they seen behavior that they wanted repeated. You can purchase a roll of tickets (carnival type) at your local store, the estimated cost is around $10.00, and provide your child's teachers with tickets too.

11. WHAT TO DO IF THEY ARE PAYING FOR INAPPROPRIATE BEHAVIOR OR MISBEHAVING. Once they reach $10.00 in negative behavior fees, give ISOLATION. Isolation in another term for grounding. Use the term ISOLATION when referring to it as a result of negative behavior. Isolation consists of staying in their room for a set amount of time that you determine with no privileges other than reading books. They receive 3 bathroom passes for 15 minutes each (use the timer). Bathroom passes are only to be used for the restroom. This is an optional idea, but I do suggest trying it if you are consistently seeing negative behaviors.
    a. In our case we use isolation in day increments, and if our children come out of the room without permission or a bathroom pass we add another day. JUST A SIDE NOTE, OUR CHILDREN HAVE BEEN IN ISOLATION ONCE EACH AND THEY CHOOSE TO NOT TO EXHIBIT THE BEHAVIOR TO RECEIVE IT AGAIN.
12. Implement the program.

Remember to set your own limits to things in your household. Our children are only allowed a coke every now and then, and they must ask for everything even if they have the money to purchase it prior to purchasing it. We do this to monitor what snacks they are eating, how much TV time they have, and such. Every household is different, the great thing about this program is that it conforms to your personal way of living.

The list "How to earn Kid Kash Money" can be modified to include items that you would like achieved, and the checkout list can be modified to include items not listed.

Please cut out pages containing Kid Kash "How to earn money", Kid Kash checkout list, Kid Kash dollar bills, and isolation passes (optional) to begin use.

How to Earn Kid Kash $$$ Money $$$

Clean the Table	$1.00
Feed Pet	$1.00
Vaccuum (Per Room)	$2.00
Sweep (Per Room)	$3.00
Dishes	$3.00
Brush Teeth	$1.00
Homework Per Page	$1.00
Read (30 Minutes at least)	$3.00
Water the Yard	$1.00
Dust Living Room	$2.00
Take out Trash	$1.00
Clean the Bathroom (toilet, sink, shower, and pick up floors)	$3.00
Grade = A	$2.00
Grade = B	$1.00
Laundry per load (wash, dry, fold)	$5.00
Bedroom includes vacuuming or cleaning floors	$5.00
Make your bed	$2.00
Bath pet	$3.00
Wash your own dishes after meals	$1.00
Get Dressed	$1.00
Brush & Fix your hair	$1.00
Mop Floors	$3.00
Put away dishes	$1.00
Help Make Dinner	$3.00
Flossing	$1.00
Good Note from Teacher	$2.00
Put on Deodorant	$1.00
Wash Car	$5.00
Put Away Clothes	$2.00

How to Earn Kid Kash $$$ Money $$$

Kid Kash Store Checkout List

Movie	$3.00
Coke	$1.00
Play Outside – 1 HR	$3.00
Play with Friends – 1 HR	$3.00
Extra Time Outside/ Friends – 1 HR	$1.00
Toy – Single	$1.00
Snack	$1.00
DS / PSP – All Day	$4.00
TV Time – 1 HR	$3.00
Movie with Mom/Dad	$5.00
Computer Time – 1 HR	$3.00
IPOD – All Day	$4.00
Playstation/ XBOX – 1 HR	$4.00
Candy	$1.00
Go to the Store (so you can shop)	$5.00
Nightlight	$1.00
Ride Bike – 1 HR	$1.00
Skateboard – 1 HR	$2.00
1 HR Past Bed Time	$1.00
Door Shut – 1 HR	$1.00
Whining	$2.00
Telling Mom/Dad NO	$2.00
LYING	$5.00
STEALING	$5.00
Mom/Dad to pick up things – per item	$1.00
Cell Phone – All Day	$4.00
Radio – All Day	$4.00
Drawing – 1 HR	$2.00
Games for PSP/DS/XBOX/Playstation – per game	$1.00
Guitar – All day	$3.00
Karaoke– 1 HR	$3.00
Naughty Note from school	$3.00
Swimming – 2 HR	$4.00
Water Toys(floats, water guns, noodles) – per item	$2.00
Interrupting	$1.00

Being Loud	$1.00
Talking with food in mouth	$1.00
Making faces because you are mad	$1.00
Obnoxious/Annoying behavior	$1.00
Inappropriate Behavior	$2.00
Sleeping IN – 1 HR	$1.00
Seconds after meal	$1.00
Day Pass with Friends	$10.00
Reminder Fee (when you have to be reminded to do items like brush teeth)	$1.00
Board Game / Cards	$3.00
Extra Hour	$1.00

Kid Kash Store Checkout Book

Date	Day of Week	Item Rented / Behavior Charge	Cost

Kid Kash Store Checkout Book

Date	Day of Week	Item Rented / Behavior Charge	Cost

Kid Kash Store Checkout Book

Date	Day of Week	Item Rented / Behavior Charge	Cost

Kid Kash Store Checkout Book

Date	Day of Week	Item Rented / Behavior Charge	Cost

Kid Kash Store Checkout Book

Date	Day of Week	Item Rented / Behavior Charge	Cost

Kid Kash Store Checkout Book

Date	Day of Week	Item Rented / Behavior Charge	Cost

Kid Kash Store Checkout Book

Date	Day of Week	Item Rented / Behavior Charge	Cost

Kid Kash Store Checkout Book

Date	Day of Week	Item Rented / Behavior Charge	Cost

Kid Kash Store Checkout Book

Date	Day of Week	Item Rented / Behavior Charge	Cost

Kid Kash Store Checkout Book

Date	Day of Week	Item Rented / Behavior Charge	Cost

Kid Kash Store Checkout Book

Date	Day of Week	Item Rented / Behavior Charge	Cost

Kid Kash Store Checkout Book

Date	Day of Week	Item Rented / Behavior Charge	Cost

Kid Kash Store Checkout Book

Date	Day of Week	Item Rented / Behavior Charge	Cost

Kid Kash Store Checkout Book

Date	Day of Week	Item Rented / Behavior Charge	Cost

Official Kid Kash Official Kid Kash

Official Kid Kash Official Kid Kash Official Kid Kash Official Kid Kash Official Kid Kash Official Kid Kash

Official Kid Kash Official Kid Kash Official Kid Kash Official Kid Kash Official Kid Kash Official Kid Kash

Official Kid Kash Official Kid Kash Official Kid Kash Official Kid Kash Official Kid Kash Official Kid Kash

Official Kid Kash Official Kid Kash Official Kid Kash Official Kid Kash Official Kid Kash Official Kid Kash

Official Kid Kash Official Kid Kash Official Kid Kash Official Kid Kash Official Kid Kash Official Kid Kash

Official Kid Kash Official Kid Kash Official Kid Kash Official Kid Kash Official Kid Kash Official Kid Kash

Official Kid Kash Official Kid Kash Official Kid Kash Official Kid Kash Official Kid Kash Official Kid Kash

Official Kid Kash Official Kid Kash Official Kid Kash Official Kid Kash Official Kid Kash Official Kid Kash

Official Kid Kash Official Kid Kash Official Kid Kash Official Kid Kash Official Kid Kash Official Kid Kash

Official Kid Kash Official Kid Kash Official Kid Kash Official Kid Kash Official Kid Kash Official Kid Kash

Official Kid Kash Official Kid Kash Official Kid Kash Official Kid Kash Official Kid Kash Official Kid Kash

Official Kid Kash Official Kid Kash Official Kid Kash Official Kid Kash Official Kid Kash Official Kid Kash

Official Kid Kash Official Kid Kash Official Kid Kash Official Kid Kash Official Kid Kash Official Kid Kash

Official Kid Kash Official Kid Kash Official Kid Kash Official Kid Kash Official Kid Kash Official Kid Kash

Official Kid Kash Official Kid Kash Official Kid Kash Official Kid Kash Official Kid Kash Official Kid Kash

Official Kid Kash Official Kid Kash Official Kid Kash Official Kid Kash Official Kid Kash Official Kid Kash

Official Kid Kash Official Kid Kash Official Kid Kash Official Kid Kash Official Kid Kash Official Kid Kash

Official Kid Kash Official Kid Kash Official Kid Kash Official Kid Kash Official Kid Kash Official Kid Kash

Official Kid Kash Official Kid Kash Official Kid Kash Official Kid Kash Official Kid Kash Official Kid Kash

Official Kid Kash Official Kid Kash Official Kid Kash Official Kid Kash Official Kid Kash Official Kid Kash

Official Kid Kash Official Kid Kash Official Kid Kash Official Kid Kash Official Kid Kash Official Kid Kash

Official Kid Kash Official Kid Kash Official Kid Kash Official Kid Kash Official Kid Kash Official Kid Kash

Official Kid Kash Official Kid Kash Official Kid Kash Official Kid Kash Official Kid Kash Official Kid Kash

Official Kid Kash Official Kid Kash Official Kid Kash Official Kid Kash Official Kid Kash Official Kid Kash

Official Kid Kash Official Kid Kash Official Kid Kash Official Kid Kash Official Kid Kash Official Kid Kash

The Kid Kash Program

Official Kid Kash Official Kid Kash Official Kid Kash Official Kid Kash Official Kid Kash Official Kid Kash

Official Kid Kash Official Kid Kash Official Kid Kash Official Kid Kash Official Kid Kash Official Kid Kash

Official Kid Kash Official Kid Kash Official Kid Kash Official Kid Kash Official Kid Kash Official Kid Kash

Official Kid Kash Official Kid Kash Official Kid Kash Official Kid Kash Official Kid Kash Official Kid Kash

Official Kid Kash Official Kid Kash Official Kid Kash Official Kid Kash Official Kid Kash Official Kid Kash

Official Kid Kash Official Kid Kash Official Kid Kash Official Kid Kash Official Kid Kash Official Kid Kash

Official Kid Kash Official Kid Kash Official Kid Kash Official Kid Kash Official Kid Kash Official Kid Kash

Official Kid Kash Official Kid Kash Official Kid Kash Official Kid Kash Official Kid Kash Official Kid Kash

Official Kid Kash Official Kid Kash Official Kid Kash Official Kid Kash Official Kid Kash Official Kid Kash

Official Kid Kash Official Kid Kash Official Kid Kash Official Kid Kash Official Kid Kash Official Kid Kash

Official Kid Kash Official Kid Kash Official Kid Kash Official Kid Kash Official Kid Kash Official Kid Kash

Official Kid Kash Official Kid Kash Official Kid Kash Official Kid Kash Official Kid Kash Official Kid Kash

Official Kid Kash Official Kid Kash Official Kid Kash Official Kid Kash Official Kid Kash Official Kid Kash

Official Kid Kash Official Kid Kash Official Kid Kash Official Kid Kash Official Kid Kash Official Kid Kash

Official Kid Kash Official Kid Kash Official Kid Kash Official Kid Kash Official Kid Kash Official Kid Kash

Official Kid Kash Official Kid Kash Official Kid Kash Official Kid Kash Official Kid Kash Official Kid Kash

Official Kid Kash Official Kid Kash Official Kid Kash Official Kid Kash Official Kid Kash Official Kid Kash

Official Kid Kash Official Kid Kash Official Kid Kash Official Kid Kash Official Kid Kash Official Kid Kash

Official Kid Kash Official Kid Kash Official Kid Kash Official Kid Kash Official Kid Kash Official Kid Kash

Official Kid Kash Official Kid Kash Official Kid Kash Official Kid Kash Official Kid Kash Official Kid Kash

Official Kid Kash Official Kid Kash Official Kid Kash Official Kid Kash Official Kid Kash Official Kid Kash

Official Kid Kash Official Kid Kash Official Kid Kash Official Kid Kash Official Kid Kash Official Kid Kash

Official Kid Kash Official Kid Kash Official Kid Kash Official Kid Kash Official Kid Kash Official Kid Kash

Official Kid Kash Official Kid Kash Official Kid Kash Official Kid Kash Official Kid Kash Official Kid Kash

Official Kid Kash Official Kid Kash Official Kid Kash Official Kid Kash Official Kid Kash Official Kid Kash

Official Kid Kash Official Kid Kash Official Kid Kash Official Kid Kash Official Kid Kash Official Kid Kash

Official Kid Kash Official Kid Kash Official Kid Kash Official Kid Kash Official Kid Kash Official Kid Kash

Official Kid Kash Official Kid Kash

Official Kid Kash Official Kid Kash Official Kid Kash Official Kid Kash Official Kid Kash Official Kid Kash

Official Kid Kash Official Kid Kash Official Kid Kash Official Kid Kash Official Kid Kash Official Kid Kash

Official Kid Kash Official Kid Kash Official Kid Kash Official Kid Kash Official Kid Kash Official Kid Kash

Official Kid Kash Official Kid Kash Official Kid Kash Official Kid Kash Official Kid Kash Official Kid Kash

Official Kid Kash Official Kid Kash Official Kid Kash Official Kid Kash Official Kid Kash Official Kid Kash

Official Kid Kash Official Kid Kash Official Kid Kash Official Kid Kash Official Kid Kash Official Kid Kash

Official Kid Kash Official Kid Kash Official Kid Kash Official Kid Kash Official Kid Kash Official Kid Kash

Official Kid Kash Official Kid Kash Official Kid Kash Official Kid Kash Official Kid Kash Official Kid Kash

Official Kid Kash Official Kid Kash Official Kid Kash Official Kid Kash Official Kid Kash Official Kid Kash

Official Kid Kash Official Kid Kash Official Kid Kash Official Kid Kash Official Kid Kash Official Kid Kash

Official Kid Kash Official Kid Kash Official Kid Kash Official Kid Kash Official Kid Kash Official Kid Kash

Official Kid Kash Official Kid Kash Official Kid Kash Official Kid Kash Official Kid Kash Official Kid Kash

Official Kid Kash Official Kid Kash Official Kid Kash Official Kid Kash Official Kid Kash Official Kid Kash

Official Kid Kash Official Kid Kash Official Kid Kash Official Kid Kash Official Kid Kash Official Kid Kash

Official Kid Kash Official Kid Kash Official Kid Kash Official Kid Kash Official Kid Kash Official Kid Kash

Official Kid Kash Official Kid Kash Official Kid Kash Official Kid Kash Official Kid Kash Official Kid Kash

Official Kid Kash Official Kid Kash Official Kid Kash Official Kid Kash Official Kid Kash Official Kid Kash

Official Kid Kash Official Kid Kash Official Kid Kash Official Kid Kash Official Kid Kash Official Kid Kash

Official Kid Kash Official Kid Kash Official Kid Kash Official Kid Kash Official Kid Kash Official Kid Kash

Official Kid Kash Official Kid Kash Official Kid Kash Official Kid Kash Official Kid Kash Official Kid Kash

Official Kid Kash Official Kid Kash Official Kid Kash Official Kid Kash Official Kid Kash Official Kid Kash

Official Kid Kash Official Kid Kash Official Kid Kash Official Kid Kash Official Kid Kash Official Kid Kash

Official Kid Kash Official Kid Kash Official Kid Kash Official Kid Kash Official Kid Kash Official Kid Kash

Official Kid Kash Official Kid Kash Official Kid Kash Official Kid Kash Official Kid Kash Official Kid Kash

Official Kid Kash Official Kid Kash Official Kid Kash Official Kid Kash Official Kid Kash Official Kid Kash

Official Kid Kash Official Kid Kash Official Kid Kash Official Kid Kash Official Kid Kash Official Kid Kash

The Kid Kash Program

Official Kid Kash Official Kid Kash

Official Kid Kash Official Kid Kash Official Kid Kash Official Kid Kash Official Kid Kash Official Kid Kash

Official Kid Kash Official Kid Kash Official Kid Kash Official Kid Kash Official Kid Kash Official Kid Kash

Official Kid Kash Official Kid Kash Official Kid Kash Official Kid Kash Official Kid Kash Official Kid Kash

Official Kid Kash Official Kid Kash Official Kid Kash Official Kid Kash Official Kid Kash Official Kid Kash

Official Kid Kash Official Kid Kash Official Kid Kash Official Kid Kash Official Kid Kash Official Kid Kash

Official Kid Kash Official Kid Kash Official Kid Kash Official Kid Kash Official Kid Kash Official Kid Kash

Official Kid Kash Official Kid Kash Official Kid Kash Official Kid Kash Official Kid Kash Official Kid Kash

Official Kid Kash Official Kid Kash Official Kid Kash Official Kid Kash Official Kid Kash Official Kid Kash

Official Kid Kash Official Kid Kash Official Kid Kash Official Kid Kash Official Kid Kash Official Kid Kash

Official Kid Kash Official Kid Kash Official Kid Kash Official Kid Kash Official Kid Kash Official Kid Kash

Official Kid Kash Official Kid Kash Official Kid Kash Official Kid Kash Official Kid Kash Official Kid Kash

Official Kid Kash Official Kid Kash Official Kid Kash Official Kid Kash Official Kid Kash Official Kid Kash

Official Kid Kash Official Kid Kash Official Kid Kash Official Kid Kash Official Kid Kash Official Kid Kash

Official Kid Kash Official Kid Kash Official Kid Kash Official Kid Kash Official Kid Kash Official Kid Kash

Official Kid Kash Official Kid Kash Official Kid Kash Official Kid Kash Official Kid Kash Official Kid Kash

Official Kid Kash Official Kid Kash Official Kid Kash Official Kid Kash Official Kid Kash Official Kid Kash

Official Kid Kash Official Kid Kash Official Kid Kash Official Kid Kash Official Kid Kash Official Kid Kash

Official Kid Kash Official Kid Kash Official Kid Kash Official Kid Kash Official Kid Kash Official Kid Kash

Official Kid Kash Official Kid Kash Official Kid Kash Official Kid Kash Official Kid Kash Official Kid Kash

Official Kid Kash Official Kid Kash Official Kid Kash Official Kid Kash Official Kid Kash Official Kid Kash

Official Kid Kash Official Kid Kash Official Kid Kash Official Kid Kash Official Kid Kash Official Kid Kash

Official Kid Kash Official Kid Kash Official Kid Kash Official Kid Kash Official Kid Kash Official Kid Kash

Official Kid Kash Official Kid Kash Official Kid Kash Official Kid Kash Official Kid Kash Official Kid Kash

Official Kid Kash Official Kid Kash Official Kid Kash Official Kid Kash Official Kid Kash Official Kid Kash

Official Kid Kash Official Kid Kash Official Kid Kash Official Kid Kash Official Kid Kash Official Kid Kash

The Kid Kash Program

Official Kid Kash Official Kid Kash Official Kid Kash Official Kid Kash Official Kid Kash Official Kid Kash

Official Kid Kash Official Kid Kash Official Kid Kash Official Kid Kash Official Kid Kash Official Kid Kash

Official Kid Kash Official Kid Kash Official Kid Kash Official Kid Kash Official Kid Kash Official Kid Kash

Official Kid Kash Official Kid Kash Official Kid Kash Official Kid Kash Official Kid Kash Official Kid Kash

Official Kid Kash Official Kid Kash Official Kid Kash Official Kid Kash Official Kid Kash Official Kid Kash

Official Kid Kash Official Kid Kash Official Kid Kash Official Kid Kash Official Kid Kash Official Kid Kash

Official Kid Kash Official Kid Kash Official Kid Kash Official Kid Kash Official Kid Kash Official Kid Kash

Official Kid Kash Official Kid Kash Official Kid Kash Official Kid Kash Official Kid Kash Official Kid Kash

Official Kid Kash Official Kid Kash Official Kid Kash Official Kid Kash Official Kid Kash Official Kid Kash

Official Kid Kash Official Kid Kash Official Kid Kash Official Kid Kash Official Kid Kash Official Kid Kash

Official Kid Kash Official Kid Kash Official Kid Kash Official Kid Kash Official Kid Kash Official Kid Kash

Official Kid Kash Official Kid Kash Official Kid Kash Official Kid Kash Official Kid Kash Official Kid Kash

Official Kid Kash Official Kid Kash Official Kid Kash Official Kid Kash Official Kid Kash Official Kid Kash

Official Kid Kash Official Kid Kash Official Kid Kash Official Kid Kash Official Kid Kash Official Kid Kash

Official Kid Kash Official Kid Kash Official Kid Kash Official Kid Kash Official Kid Kash Official Kid Kash

Official Kid Kash Official Kid Kash Official Kid Kash Official Kid Kash Official Kid Kash Official Kid Kash

Official Kid Kash Official Kid Kash Official Kid Kash Official Kid Kash Official Kid Kash Official Kid Kash

Official Kid Kash Official Kid Kash Official Kid Kash Official Kid Kash Official Kid Kash Official Kid Kash

Official Kid Kash Official Kid Kash Official Kid Kash Official Kid Kash Official Kid Kash Official Kid Kash

Official Kid Kash Official Kid Kash Official Kid Kash Official Kid Kash Official Kid Kash Official Kid Kash

Official Kid Kash Official Kid Kash Official Kid Kash Official Kid Kash Official Kid Kash Official Kid Kash

Official Kid Kash Official Kid Kash Official Kid Kash Official Kid Kash Official Kid Kash Official Kid Kash

Official Kid Kash Official Kid Kash Official Kid Kash Official Kid Kash Official Kid Kash Official Kid Kash

Official Kid Kash Official Kid Kash Official Kid Kash Official Kid Kash Official Kid Kash Official Kid Kash

Official Kid Kash Official Kid Kash Official Kid Kash Official Kid Kash Official Kid Kash Official Kid Kash

Official Kid Kash Official Kid Kash Official Kid Kash Official Kid Kash Official Kid Kash Official Kid Kash

Official Kid Kash Official Kid Kash Official Kid Kash Official Kid Kash Official Kid Kash Official Kid Kash
Official Kid Kash Official Kid Kash Official Kid Kash Official Kid Kash Official Kid Kash Official Kid Kash
Official Kid Kash Official Kid Kash Official Kid Kash Official Kid Kash Official Kid Kash Official Kid Kash
Official Kid Kash Official Kid Kash Official Kid Kash Official Kid Kash Official Kid Kash Official Kid Kash
Official Kid Kash Official Kid Kash Official Kid Kash Official Kid Kash Official Kid Kash Official Kid Kash
Official Kid Kash Official Kid Kash Official Kid Kash Official Kid Kash Official Kid Kash Official Kid Kash
Official Kid Kash Official Kid Kash Official Kid Kash Official Kid Kash Official Kid Kash Official Kid Kash
Official Kid Kash Official Kid Kash Official Kid Kash Official Kid Kash Official Kid Kash Official Kid Kash
Official Kid Kash Official Kid Kash Official Kid Kash Official Kid Kash Official Kid Kash Official Kid Kash
Official Kid Kash Official Kid Kash Official Kid Kash Official Kid Kash Official Kid Kash Official Kid Kash
Official Kid Kash Official Kid Kash Official Kid Kash Official Kid Kash Official Kid Kash Official Kid Kash
Official Kid Kash Official Kid Kash Official Kid Kash Official Kid Kash Official Kid Kash Official Kid Kash
Official Kid Kash Official Kid Kash Official Kid Kash Official Kid Kash Official Kid Kash Official Kid Kash
Official Kid Kash Official Kid Kash Official Kid Kash Official Kid Kash Official Kid Kash Official Kid Kash
Official Kid Kash Official Kid Kash Official Kid Kash Official Kid Kash Official Kid Kash Official Kid Kash
Official Kid Kash Official Kid Kash Official Kid Kash Official Kid Kash Official Kid Kash Official Kid Kash
Official Kid Kash Official Kid Kash Official Kid Kash Official Kid Kash Official Kid Kash Official Kid Kash
Official Kid Kash Official Kid Kash Official Kid Kash Official Kid Kash Official Kid Kash Official Kid Kash
Official Kid Kash Official Kid Kash Official Kid Kash Official Kid Kash Official Kid Kash Official Kid Kash
Official Kid Kash Official Kid Kash Official Kid Kash Official Kid Kash Official Kid Kash Official Kid Kash
Official Kid Kash Official Kid Kash Official Kid Kash Official Kid Kash Official Kid Kash Official Kid Kash
Official Kid Kash Official Kid Kash Official Kid Kash Official Kid Kash Official Kid Kash Official Kid Kash
Official Kid Kash Official Kid Kash Official Kid Kash Official Kid Kash Official Kid Kash Official Kid Kash
Official Kid Kash Official Kid Kash Official Kid Kash Official Kid Kash Official Kid Kash Official Kid Kash
Official Kid Kash Official Kid Kash Official Kid Kash Official Kid Kash Official Kid Kash Official Kid Kash
Official Kid Kash Official Kid Kash Official Kid Kash Official Kid Kash Official Kid Kash Official Kid Kash
Official Kid Kash Official Kid Kash Official Kid Kash Official Kid Kash Official Kid Kash Official Kid Kash
Official Kid Kash Official Kid Kash Official Kid Kash Official Kid Kash Official Kid Kash Official Kid Kash

The Kid Kash Program

Official Kid Kash Official Kid Kash Official Kid Kash Official Kid Kash Official Kid Kash Official Kid Kash

Official Kid Kash Official Kid Kash Official Kid Kash Official Kid Kash Official Kid Kash Official Kid Kash

Official Kid Kash Official Kid Kash Official Kid Kash Official Kid Kash Official Kid Kash Official Kid Kash

Official Kid Kash Official Kid Kash Official Kid Kash Official Kid Kash Official Kid Kash Official Kid Kash

Official Kid Kash Official Kid Kash Official Kid Kash Official Kid Kash Official Kid Kash Official Kid Kash

Official Kid Kash Official Kid Kash Official Kid Kash Official Kid Kash Official Kid Kash Official Kid Kash

Official Kid Kash Official Kid Kash Official Kid Kash Official Kid Kash Official Kid Kash Official Kid Kash

Official Kid Kash Official Kid Kash Official Kid Kash Official Kid Kash Official Kid Kash Official Kid Kash

Official Kid Kash Official Kid Kash Official Kid Kash Official Kid Kash Official Kid Kash Official Kid Kash

Official Kid Kash Official Kid Kash Official Kid Kash Official Kid Kash Official Kid Kash Official Kid Kash

Official Kid Kash Official Kid Kash Official Kid Kash Official Kid Kash Official Kid Kash Official Kid Kash

Official Kid Kash Official Kid Kash Official Kid Kash Official Kid Kash Official Kid Kash Official Kid Kash

Official Kid Kash Official Kid Kash Official Kid Kash Official Kid Kash Official Kid Kash Official Kid Kash

Official Kid Kash Official Kid Kash Official Kid Kash Official Kid Kash Official Kid Kash Official Kid Kash

Official Kid Kash Official Kid Kash Official Kid Kash Official Kid Kash Official Kid Kash Official Kid Kash

Official Kid Kash Official Kid Kash Official Kid Kash Official Kid Kash Official Kid Kash Official Kid Kash

Official Kid Kash Official Kid Kash Official Kid Kash Official Kid Kash Official Kid Kash Official Kid Kash

Official Kid Kash Official Kid Kash Official Kid Kash Official Kid Kash Official Kid Kash Official Kid Kash

Official Kid Kash Official Kid Kash Official Kid Kash Official Kid Kash Official Kid Kash Official Kid Kash

Official Kid Kash Official Kid Kash Official Kid Kash Official Kid Kash Official Kid Kash Official Kid Kash

Official Kid Kash Official Kid Kash Official Kid Kash Official Kid Kash Official Kid Kash Official Kid Kash

Official Kid Kash Official Kid Kash Official Kid Kash Official Kid Kash Official Kid Kash Official Kid Kash

Official Kid Kash Official Kid Kash Official Kid Kash Official Kid Kash Official Kid Kash Official Kid Kash

Official Kid Kash Official Kid Kash Official Kid Kash Official Kid Kash Official Kid Kash Official Kid Kash

Official Kid Kash Official Kid Kash Official Kid Kash Official Kid Kash Official Kid Kash Official Kid Kash

Official Kid Kash Official Kid Kash Official Kid Kash Official Kid Kash Official Kid Kash Official Kid Kash

Official Kid Kash Official Kid Kash Official Kid Kash Official Kid Kash Official Kid Kash Official Kid Kash
Official Kid Kash Official Kid Kash Official Kid Kash Official Kid Kash Official Kid Kash Official Kid Kash
Official Kid Kash Official Kid Kash Official Kid Kash Official Kid Kash Official Kid Kash Official Kid Kash
Official Kid Kash Official Kid Kash Official Kid Kash Official Kid Kash Official Kid Kash Official Kid Kash
Official Kid Kash Official Kid Kash Official Kid Kash Official Kid Kash Official Kid Kash Official Kid Kash
Official Kid Kash Official Kid Kash Official Kid Kash Official Kid Kash Official Kid Kash Official Kid Kash
Official Kid Kash Official Kid Kash Official Kid Kash Official Kid Kash Official Kid Kash Official Kid Kash
Official Kid Kash Official Kid Kash Official Kid Kash Official Kid Kash Official Kid Kash Official Kid Kash
Official Kid Kash Official Kid Kash Official Kid Kash Official Kid Kash Official Kid Kash Official Kid Kash
Official Kid Kash Official Kid Kash Official Kid Kash Official Kid Kash Official Kid Kash Official Kid Kash
Official Kid Kash Official Kid Kash Official Kid Kash Official Kid Kash Official Kid Kash Official Kid Kash
Official Kid Kash Official Kid Kash Official Kid Kash Official Kid Kash Official Kid Kash Official Kid Kash
Official Kid Kash Official Kid Kash Official Kid Kash Official Kid Kash Official Kid Kash Official Kid Kash
Official Kid Kash Official Kid Kash Official Kid Kash Official Kid Kash Official Kid Kash Official Kid Kash
Official Kid Kash Official Kid Kash Official Kid Kash Official Kid Kash Official Kid Kash Official Kid Kash
Official Kid Kash Official Kid Kash Official Kid Kash Official Kid Kash Official Kid Kash Official Kid Kash
Official Kid Kash Official Kid Kash Official Kid Kash Official Kid Kash Official Kid Kash Official Kid Kash
Official Kid Kash Official Kid Kash Official Kid Kash Official Kid Kash Official Kid Kash Official Kid Kash
Official Kid Kash Official Kid Kash Official Kid Kash Official Kid Kash Official Kid Kash Official Kid Kash
Official Kid Kash Official Kid Kash Official Kid Kash Official Kid Kash Official Kid Kash Official Kid Kash
Official Kid Kash Official Kid Kash Official Kid Kash Official Kid Kash Official Kid Kash Official Kid Kash
Official Kid Kash Official Kid Kash Official Kid Kash Official Kid Kash Official Kid Kash Official Kid Kash
Official Kid Kash Official Kid Kash Official Kid Kash Official Kid Kash Official Kid Kash Official Kid Kash
Official Kid Kash Official Kid Kash Official Kid Kash Official Kid Kash Official Kid Kash Official Kid Kash
Official Kid Kash Official Kid Kash Official Kid Kash Official Kid Kash Official Kid Kash Official Kid Kash
Official Kid Kash Official Kid Kash Official Kid Kash Official Kid Kash Official Kid Kash Official Kid Kash

The Kid Kash Program

Official Kid Kash Official Kid Kash Official Kid Kash Official Kid Kash Official Kid Kash Official Kid Kash

Official Kid Kash Official Kid Kash Official Kid Kash Official Kid Kash Official Kid Kash Official Kid Kash

Official Kid Kash Official Kid Kash Official Kid Kash Official Kid Kash Official Kid Kash Official Kid Kash

Official Kid Kash Official Kid Kash Official Kid Kash Official Kid Kash Official Kid Kash Official Kid Kash

Official Kid Kash Official Kid Kash Official Kid Kash Official Kid Kash Official Kid Kash Official Kid Kash

Official Kid Kash Official Kid Kash Official Kid Kash Official Kid Kash Official Kid Kash Official Kid Kash

Official Kid Kash Official Kid Kash Official Kid Kash Official Kid Kash Official Kid Kash Official Kid Kash

Official Kid Kash Official Kid Kash Official Kid Kash Official Kid Kash Official Kid Kash Official Kid Kash

Official Kid Kash Official Kid Kash Official Kid Kash Official Kid Kash Official Kid Kash Official Kid Kash

Official Kid Kash Official Kid Kash Official Kid Kash Official Kid Kash Official Kid Kash Official Kid Kash

Official Kid Kash Official Kid Kash Official Kid Kash Official Kid Kash Official Kid Kash Official Kid Kash

Official Kid Kash Official Kid Kash Official Kid Kash Official Kid Kash Official Kid Kash Official Kid Kash

Official Kid Kash Official Kid Kash Official Kid Kash Official Kid Kash Official Kid Kash Official Kid Kash

Official Kid Kash Official Kid Kash Official Kid Kash Official Kid Kash Official Kid Kash Official Kid Kash

Official Kid Kash Official Kid Kash Official Kid Kash Official Kid Kash Official Kid Kash Official Kid Kash

Official Kid Kash Official Kid Kash Official Kid Kash Official Kid Kash Official Kid Kash Official Kid Kash

Official Kid Kash Official Kid Kash Official Kid Kash Official Kid Kash Official Kid Kash Official Kid Kash

Official Kid Kash Official Kid Kash Official Kid Kash Official Kid Kash Official Kid Kash Official Kid Kash

Official Kid Kash Official Kid Kash Official Kid Kash Official Kid Kash Official Kid Kash Official Kid Kash

Official Kid Kash Official Kid Kash Official Kid Kash Official Kid Kash Official Kid Kash Official Kid Kash

Official Kid Kash Official Kid Kash Official Kid Kash Official Kid Kash Official Kid Kash Official Kid Kash

Official Kid Kash Official Kid Kash Official Kid Kash Official Kid Kash Official Kid Kash Official Kid Kash

Official Kid Kash Official Kid Kash Official Kid Kash Official Kid Kash Official Kid Kash Official Kid Kash

Official Kid Kash Official Kid Kash Official Kid Kash Official Kid Kash Official Kid Kash Official Kid Kash

Official Kid Kash Official Kid Kash Official Kid Kash Official Kid Kash Official Kid Kash Official Kid Kash

Official Kid Kash Official Kid Kash Official Kid Kash Official Kid Kash Official Kid Kash Official Kid Kash

The Kid Kash Program

Official Kid Kash Official Kid Kash

The Kid Kash Program

Official Kid Kash Official Kid Kash Official Kid Kash Official Kid Kash Official Kid Kash Official Kid Kash

Official Kid Kash Official Kid Kash Official Kid Kash Official Kid Kash Official Kid Kash Official Kid Kash

Official Kid Kash Official Kid Kash Official Kid Kash Official Kid Kash Official Kid Kash Official Kid Kash

Official Kid Kash Official Kid Kash Official Kid Kash Official Kid Kash Official Kid Kash Official Kid Kash

Official Kid Kash Official Kid Kash Official Kid Kash Official Kid Kash Official Kid Kash Official Kid Kash

Official Kid Kash Official Kid Kash Official Kid Kash Official Kid Kash Official Kid Kash Official Kid Kash

Official Kid Kash Official Kid Kash Official Kid Kash Official Kid Kash Official Kid Kash Official Kid Kash

Official Kid Kash Official Kid Kash Official Kid Kash Official Kid Kash Official Kid Kash Official Kid Kash

Official Kid Kash Official Kid Kash Official Kid Kash Official Kid Kash Official Kid Kash Official Kid Kash

Official Kid Kash Official Kid Kash Official Kid Kash Official Kid Kash Official Kid Kash Official Kid Kash

Official Kid Kash Official Kid Kash Official Kid Kash Official Kid Kash Official Kid Kash Official Kid Kash

Official Kid Kash Official Kid Kash Official Kid Kash Official Kid Kash Official Kid Kash Official Kid Kash

Official Kid Kash Official Kid Kash Official Kid Kash Official Kid Kash Official Kid Kash Official Kid Kash

Official Kid Kash Official Kid Kash Official Kid Kash Official Kid Kash Official Kid Kash Official Kid Kash

Official Kid Kash Official Kid Kash Official Kid Kash Official Kid Kash Official Kid Kash Official Kid Kash

Official Kid Kash Official Kid Kash Official Kid Kash Official Kid Kash Official Kid Kash Official Kid Kash

Official Kid Kash Official Kid Kash Official Kid Kash Official Kid Kash Official Kid Kash Official Kid Kash

Official Kid Kash Official Kid Kash Official Kid Kash Official Kid Kash Official Kid Kash Official Kid Kash

Official Kid Kash Official Kid Kash Official Kid Kash Official Kid Kash Official Kid Kash Official Kid Kash

Official Kid Kash Official Kid Kash Official Kid Kash Official Kid Kash Official Kid Kash Official Kid Kash

Official Kid Kash Official Kid Kash Official Kid Kash Official Kid Kash Official Kid Kash Official Kid Kash

Official Kid Kash Official Kid Kash Official Kid Kash Official Kid Kash Official Kid Kash Official Kid Kash

Official Kid Kash Official Kid Kash Official Kid Kash Official Kid Kash Official Kid Kash Official Kid Kash

Official Kid Kash Official Kid Kash Official Kid Kash Official Kid Kash Official Kid Kash Official Kid Kash

Official Kid Kash Official Kid Kash Official Kid Kash Official Kid Kash Official Kid Kash Official Kid Kash

Official Kid Kash Official Kid Kash Official Kid Kash Official Kid Kash Official Kid Kash Official Kid Kash

Official Kid Kash Official Kid Kash Official Kid Kash Official Kid Kash Official Kid Kash Official Kid Kash

Official Kid Kash Official Kid Kash Official Kid Kash Official Kid Kash Official Kid Kash Official Kid Kash
Official Kid Kash Official Kid Kash Official Kid Kash Official Kid Kash Official Kid Kash Official Kid Kash
Official Kid Kash Official Kid Kash Official Kid Kash Official Kid Kash Official Kid Kash Official Kid Kash
Official Kid Kash Official Kid Kash Official Kid Kash Official Kid Kash Official Kid Kash Official Kid Kash
Official Kid Kash Official Kid Kash Official Kid Kash Official Kid Kash Official Kid Kash Official Kid Kash
Official Kid Kash Official Kid Kash Official Kid Kash Official Kid Kash Official Kid Kash Official Kid Kash
Official Kid Kash Official Kid Kash Official Kid Kash Official Kid Kash Official Kid Kash Official Kid Kash
Official Kid Kash Official Kid Kash Official Kid Kash Official Kid Kash Official Kid Kash Official Kid Kash
Official Kid Kash Official Kid Kash Official Kid Kash Official Kid Kash Official Kid Kash Official Kid Kash
Official Kid Kash Official Kid Kash Official Kid Kash Official Kid Kash Official Kid Kash Official Kid Kash
Official Kid Kash Official Kid Kash Official Kid Kash Official Kid Kash Official Kid Kash Official Kid Kash
Official Kid Kash Official Kid Kash Official Kid Kash Official Kid Kash Official Kid Kash Official Kid Kash
Official Kid Kash Official Kid Kash Official Kid Kash Official Kid Kash Official Kid Kash Official Kid Kash
Official Kid Kash Official Kid Kash Official Kid Kash Official Kid Kash Official Kid Kash Official Kid Kash
Official Kid Kash Official Kid Kash Official Kid Kash Official Kid Kash Official Kid Kash Official Kid Kash
Official Kid Kash Official Kid Kash Official Kid Kash Official Kid Kash Official Kid Kash Official Kid Kash
Official Kid Kash Official Kid Kash Official Kid Kash Official Kid Kash Official Kid Kash Official Kid Kash
Official Kid Kash Official Kid Kash Official Kid Kash Official Kid Kash Official Kid Kash Official Kid Kash
Official Kid Kash Official Kid Kash Official Kid Kash Official Kid Kash Official Kid Kash Official Kid Kash
Official Kid Kash Official Kid Kash Official Kid Kash Official Kid Kash Official Kid Kash Official Kid Kash
Official Kid Kash Official Kid Kash Official Kid Kash Official Kid Kash Official Kid Kash Official Kid Kash
Official Kid Kash Official Kid Kash Official Kid Kash Official Kid Kash Official Kid Kash Official Kid Kash
Official Kid Kash Official Kid Kash Official Kid Kash Official Kid Kash Official Kid Kash Official Kid Kash
Official Kid Kash Official Kid Kash Official Kid Kash Official Kid Kash Official Kid Kash Official Kid Kash
Official Kid Kash Official Kid Kash Official Kid Kash Official Kid Kash Official Kid Kash Official Kid Kash
Official Kid Kash Official Kid Kash Official Kid Kash Official Kid Kash Official Kid Kash Official Kid Kash
Official Kid Kash Official Kid Kash Official Kid Kash Official Kid Kash Official Kid Kash Official Kid Kash

Official Kid Kash Official Kid Kash

Official Kid Kash Official Kid Kash Official Kid Kash Official Kid Kash Official Kid Kash Official Kid Kash
Official Kid Kash Official Kid Kash Official Kid Kash Official Kid Kash Official Kid Kash Official Kid Kash
Official Kid Kash Official Kid Kash Official Kid Kash Official Kid Kash Official Kid Kash Official Kid Kash
Official Kid Kash Official Kid Kash Official Kid Kash Official Kid Kash Official Kid Kash Official Kid Kash
Official Kid Kash Official Kid Kash Official Kid Kash Official Kid Kash Official Kid Kash Official Kid Kash
Official Kid Kash Official Kid Kash Official Kid Kash Official Kid Kash Official Kid Kash Official Kid Kash
Official Kid Kash Official Kid Kash Official Kid Kash Official Kid Kash Official Kid Kash Official Kid Kash
Official Kid Kash Official Kid Kash Official Kid Kash Official Kid Kash Official Kid Kash Official Kid Kash
Official Kid Kash Official Kid Kash Official Kid Kash Official Kid Kash Official Kid Kash Official Kid Kash
Official Kid Kash Official Kid Kash Official Kid Kash Official Kid Kash Official Kid Kash Official Kid Kash
Official Kid Kash Official Kid Kash Official Kid Kash Official Kid Kash Official Kid Kash Official Kid Kash
Official Kid Kash Official Kid Kash Official Kid Kash Official Kid Kash Official Kid Kash Official Kid Kash
Official Kid Kash Official Kid Kash Official Kid Kash Official Kid Kash Official Kid Kash Official Kid Kash
Official Kid Kash Official Kid Kash Official Kid Kash Official Kid Kash Official Kid Kash Official Kid Kash
Official Kid Kash Official Kid Kash Official Kid Kash Official Kid Kash Official Kid Kash Official Kid Kash
Official Kid Kash Official Kid Kash Official Kid Kash Official Kid Kash Official Kid Kash Official Kid Kash
Official Kid Kash Official Kid Kash Official Kid Kash Official Kid Kash Official Kid Kash Official Kid Kash
Official Kid Kash Official Kid Kash Official Kid Kash Official Kid Kash Official Kid Kash Official Kid Kash
Official Kid Kash Official Kid Kash Official Kid Kash Official Kid Kash Official Kid Kash Official Kid Kash
Official Kid Kash Official Kid Kash Official Kid Kash Official Kid Kash Official Kid Kash Official Kid Kash
Official Kid Kash Official Kid Kash Official Kid Kash Official Kid Kash Official Kid Kash Official Kid Kash
Official Kid Kash Official Kid Kash Official Kid Kash Official Kid Kash Official Kid Kash Official Kid Kash
Official Kid Kash Official Kid Kash Official Kid Kash Official Kid Kash Official Kid Kash Official Kid Kash
Official Kid Kash Official Kid Kash Official Kid Kash Official Kid Kash Official Kid Kash Official Kid Kash
Official Kid Kash Official Kid Kash Official Kid Kash Official Kid Kash Official Kid Kash Official Kid Kash
Official Kid Kash Official Kid Kash Official Kid Kash Official Kid Kash Official Kid Kash Official Kid Kash

The Kid Kash Program

Official Kid Kash Official Kid Kash Official Kid Kash Official Kid Kash Official Kid Kash Official Kid Kash

Official Kid Kash Official Kid Kash Official Kid Kash Official Kid Kash Official Kid Kash Official Kid Kash

Official Kid Kash Official Kid Kash Official Kid Kash Official Kid Kash Official Kid Kash Official Kid Kash

Official Kid Kash Official Kid Kash Official Kid Kash Official Kid Kash Official Kid Kash Official Kid Kash

Official Kid Kash Official Kid Kash Official Kid Kash Official Kid Kash Official Kid Kash Official Kid Kash

Official Kid Kash Official Kid Kash Official Kid Kash Official Kid Kash Official Kid Kash Official Kid Kash

Official Kid Kash Official Kid Kash Official Kid Kash Official Kid Kash Official Kid Kash Official Kid Kash

Official Kid Kash Official Kid Kash Official Kid Kash Official Kid Kash Official Kid Kash Official Kid Kash

Official Kid Kash Official Kid Kash Official Kid Kash Official Kid Kash Official Kid Kash Official Kid Kash

Official Kid Kash Official Kid Kash Official Kid Kash Official Kid Kash Official Kid Kash Official Kid Kash

Official Kid Kash Official Kid Kash Official Kid Kash Official Kid Kash Official Kid Kash Official Kid Kash

Official Kid Kash Official Kid Kash Official Kid Kash Official Kid Kash Official Kid Kash Official Kid Kash

Official Kid Kash Official Kid Kash Official Kid Kash Official Kid Kash Official Kid Kash Official Kid Kash

Official Kid Kash Official Kid Kash Official Kid Kash Official Kid Kash Official Kid Kash Official Kid Kash

Official Kid Kash Official Kid Kash Official Kid Kash Official Kid Kash Official Kid Kash Official Kid Kash

Official Kid Kash Official Kid Kash Official Kid Kash Official Kid Kash Official Kid Kash Official Kid Kash

Official Kid Kash Official Kid Kash Official Kid Kash Official Kid Kash Official Kid Kash Official Kid Kash

Official Kid Kash Official Kid Kash Official Kid Kash Official Kid Kash Official Kid Kash Official Kid Kash

Official Kid Kash Official Kid Kash Official Kid Kash Official Kid Kash Official Kid Kash Official Kid Kash

Official Kid Kash Official Kid Kash Official Kid Kash Official Kid Kash Official Kid Kash Official Kid Kash

Official Kid Kash Official Kid Kash Official Kid Kash Official Kid Kash Official Kid Kash Official Kid Kash

Official Kid Kash Official Kid Kash Official Kid Kash Official Kid Kash Official Kid Kash Official Kid Kash

Official Kid Kash Official Kid Kash Official Kid Kash Official Kid Kash Official Kid Kash Official Kid Kash

Official Kid Kash Official Kid Kash Official Kid Kash Official Kid Kash Official Kid Kash Official Kid Kash

Official Kid Kash Official Kid Kash Official Kid Kash Official Kid Kash Official Kid Kash Official Kid Kash

Official Kid Kash Official Kid Kash Official Kid Kash Official Kid Kash Official Kid Kash Official Kid Kash

Official Kid Kash Official Kid Kash Official Kid Kash Official Kid Kash Official Kid Kash Official Kid Kash

Official Kid Kash Official Kid Kash Official Kid Kash Official Kid Kash Official Kid Kash Official Kid Kash

Official Kid Kash Official Kid Kash Official Kid Kash Official Kid Kash Official Kid Kash Official Kid Kash

Official Kid Kash Official Kid Kash Official Kid Kash Official Kid Kash Official Kid Kash Official Kid Kash

Official Kid Kash Official Kid Kash Official Kid Kash Official Kid Kash Official Kid Kash Official Kid Kash

Official Kid Kash Official Kid Kash Official Kid Kash Official Kid Kash Official Kid Kash Official Kid Kash

Official Kid Kash Official Kid Kash Official Kid Kash Official Kid Kash Official Kid Kash Official Kid Kash

Official Kid Kash Official Kid Kash Official Kid Kash Official Kid Kash Official Kid Kash Official Kid Kash

Official Kid Kash Official Kid Kash Official Kid Kash Official Kid Kash Official Kid Kash Official Kid Kash

Official Kid Kash Official Kid Kash Official Kid Kash Official Kid Kash Official Kid Kash Official Kid Kash

Official Kid Kash Official Kid Kash Official Kid Kash Official Kid Kash Official Kid Kash Official Kid Kash

Official Kid Kash Official Kid Kash Official Kid Kash Official Kid Kash Official Kid Kash Official Kid Kash

Official Kid Kash Official Kid Kash Official Kid Kash Official Kid Kash Official Kid Kash Official Kid Kash

Official Kid Kash Official Kid Kash Official Kid Kash Official Kid Kash Official Kid Kash Official Kid Kash

Official Kid Kash Official Kid Kash Official Kid Kash Official Kid Kash Official Kid Kash Official Kid Kash

Official Kid Kash Official Kid Kash Official Kid Kash Official Kid Kash Official Kid Kash Official Kid Kash

Official Kid Kash Official Kid Kash Official Kid Kash Official Kid Kash Official Kid Kash Official Kid Kash

Official Kid Kash Official Kid Kash Official Kid Kash Official Kid Kash Official Kid Kash Official Kid Kash

Official Kid Kash Official Kid Kash Official Kid Kash Official Kid Kash Official Kid Kash Official Kid Kash

Official Kid Kash Official Kid Kash Official Kid Kash Official Kid Kash Official Kid Kash Official Kid Kash

Official Kid Kash Official Kid Kash Official Kid Kash Official Kid Kash Official Kid Kash Official Kid Kash

Official Kid Kash Official Kid Kash Official Kid Kash Official Kid Kash Official Kid Kash Official Kid Kash

Official Kid Kash Official Kid Kash Official Kid Kash Official Kid Kash Official Kid Kash Official Kid Kash

Official Kid Kash Official Kid Kash Official Kid Kash Official Kid Kash Official Kid Kash Official Kid Kash

Official Kid Kash Official Kid Kash Official Kid Kash Official Kid Kash Official Kid Kash Official Kid Kash

Official Kid Kash Official Kid Kash Official Kid Kash Official Kid Kash Official Kid Kash Official Kid Kash

Official Kid Kash Official Kid Kash

The Kid Kash Program

Official Kid Kash Official Kid Kash Official Kid Kash Official Kid Kash Official Kid Kash Official Kid Kash

Official Kid Kash Official Kid Kash Official Kid Kash Official Kid Kash Official Kid Kash Official Kid Kash

Official Kid Kash Official Kid Kash Official Kid Kash Official Kid Kash Official Kid Kash Official Kid Kash

Official Kid Kash Official Kid Kash Official Kid Kash Official Kid Kash Official Kid Kash Official Kid Kash

Official Kid Kash Official Kid Kash Official Kid Kash Official Kid Kash Official Kid Kash Official Kid Kash

Official Kid Kash Official Kid Kash Official Kid Kash Official Kid Kash Official Kid Kash Official Kid Kash

Official Kid Kash Official Kid Kash Official Kid Kash Official Kid Kash Official Kid Kash Official Kid Kash

Official Kid Kash Official Kid Kash Official Kid Kash Official Kid Kash Official Kid Kash Official Kid Kash

Official Kid Kash Official Kid Kash Official Kid Kash Official Kid Kash Official Kid Kash Official Kid Kash

Official Kid Kash Official Kid Kash Official Kid Kash Official Kid Kash Official Kid Kash Official Kid Kash

Official Kid Kash Official Kid Kash Official Kid Kash Official Kid Kash Official Kid Kash Official Kid Kash

Official Kid Kash Official Kid Kash Official Kid Kash Official Kid Kash Official Kid Kash Official Kid Kash

Official Kid Kash Official Kid Kash Official Kid Kash Official Kid Kash Official Kid Kash Official Kid Kash

Official Kid Kash Official Kid Kash Official Kid Kash Official Kid Kash Official Kid Kash Official Kid Kash

Official Kid Kash Official Kid Kash Official Kid Kash Official Kid Kash Official Kid Kash Official Kid Kash

Official Kid Kash Official Kid Kash Official Kid Kash Official Kid Kash Official Kid Kash Official Kid Kash

Official Kid Kash Official Kid Kash Official Kid Kash Official Kid Kash Official Kid Kash Official Kid Kash

Official Kid Kash Official Kid Kash Official Kid Kash Official Kid Kash Official Kid Kash Official Kid Kash

Official Kid Kash Official Kid Kash Official Kid Kash Official Kid Kash Official Kid Kash Official Kid Kash

Official Kid Kash Official Kid Kash Official Kid Kash Official Kid Kash Official Kid Kash Official Kid Kash

Official Kid Kash Official Kid Kash Official Kid Kash Official Kid Kash Official Kid Kash Official Kid Kash

Official Kid Kash Official Kid Kash Official Kid Kash Official Kid Kash Official Kid Kash Official Kid Kash

Official Kid Kash Official Kid Kash Official Kid Kash Official Kid Kash Official Kid Kash Official Kid Kash

Official Kid Kash Official Kid Kash Official Kid Kash Official Kid Kash Official Kid Kash Official Kid Kash

Official Kid Kash Official Kid Kash Official Kid Kash Official Kid Kash Official Kid Kash Official Kid Kash

Official Kid Kash Official Kid Kash Official Kid Kash Official Kid Kash Official Kid Kash Official Kid Kash

The Kid Kash Program

Official Kid Kash Official Kid Kash Official Kid Kash Official Kid Kash Official Kid Kash Official Kid Kash

Official Kid Kash Official Kid Kash Official Kid Kash Official Kid Kash Official Kid Kash Official Kid Kash

Official Kid Kash Official Kid Kash Official Kid Kash Official Kid Kash Official Kid Kash Official Kid Kash

Official Kid Kash Official Kid Kash Official Kid Kash Official Kid Kash Official Kid Kash Official Kid Kash

Official Kid Kash Official Kid Kash Official Kid Kash Official Kid Kash Official Kid Kash Official Kid Kash

Official Kid Kash Official Kid Kash Official Kid Kash Official Kid Kash Official Kid Kash Official Kid Kash

Official Kid Kash Official Kid Kash Official Kid Kash Official Kid Kash Official Kid Kash Official Kid Kash

Official Kid Kash Official Kid Kash Official Kid Kash Official Kid Kash Official Kid Kash Official Kid Kash

Official Kid Kash Official Kid Kash Official Kid Kash Official Kid Kash Official Kid Kash Official Kid Kash

Official Kid Kash Official Kid Kash Official Kid Kash Official Kid Kash Official Kid Kash Official Kid Kash

Official Kid Kash Official Kid Kash Official Kid Kash Official Kid Kash Official Kid Kash Official Kid Kash

Official Kid Kash Official Kid Kash Official Kid Kash Official Kid Kash Official Kid Kash Official Kid Kash

Official Kid Kash Official Kid Kash Official Kid Kash Official Kid Kash Official Kid Kash Official Kid Kash

Official Kid Kash Official Kid Kash Official Kid Kash Official Kid Kash Official Kid Kash Official Kid Kash

Official Kid Kash Official Kid Kash Official Kid Kash Official Kid Kash Official Kid Kash Official Kid Kash

Official Kid Kash Official Kid Kash Official Kid Kash Official Kid Kash Official Kid Kash Official Kid Kash

Official Kid Kash Official Kid Kash Official Kid Kash Official Kid Kash Official Kid Kash Official Kid Kash

Official Kid Kash Official Kid Kash Official Kid Kash Official Kid Kash Official Kid Kash Official Kid Kash

Official Kid Kash Official Kid Kash Official Kid Kash Official Kid Kash Official Kid Kash Official Kid Kash

Official Kid Kash Official Kid Kash Official Kid Kash Official Kid Kash Official Kid Kash Official Kid Kash

Official Kid Kash Official Kid Kash Official Kid Kash Official Kid Kash Official Kid Kash Official Kid Kash

Official Kid Kash Official Kid Kash Official Kid Kash Official Kid Kash Official Kid Kash Official Kid Kash

Official Kid Kash Official Kid Kash Official Kid Kash Official Kid Kash Official Kid Kash Official Kid Kash

Official Kid Kash Official Kid Kash Official Kid Kash Official Kid Kash Official Kid Kash Official Kid Kash

Official Kid Kash Official Kid Kash Official Kid Kash Official Kid Kash Official Kid Kash Official Kid Kash

The Kid Kash Program

Official Kid Kash Official Kid Kash Official Kid Kash Official Kid Kash Official Kid Kash Official Kid Kash

Official Kid Kash Official Kid Kash Official Kid Kash Official Kid Kash Official Kid Kash Official Kid Kash

Official Kid Kash Official Kid Kash Official Kid Kash Official Kid Kash Official Kid Kash Official Kid Kash

Official Kid Kash Official Kid Kash Official Kid Kash Official Kid Kash Official Kid Kash Official Kid Kash

Official Kid Kash Official Kid Kash Official Kid Kash Official Kid Kash Official Kid Kash Official Kid Kash

Official Kid Kash Official Kid Kash Official Kid Kash Official Kid Kash Official Kid Kash Official Kid Kash

Official Kid Kash Official Kid Kash Official Kid Kash Official Kid Kash Official Kid Kash Official Kid Kash

Official Kid Kash Official Kid Kash Official Kid Kash Official Kid Kash Official Kid Kash Official Kid Kash

Official Kid Kash Official Kid Kash Official Kid Kash Official Kid Kash Official Kid Kash Official Kid Kash

Official Kid Kash Official Kid Kash Official Kid Kash Official Kid Kash Official Kid Kash Official Kid Kash

Official Kid Kash Official Kid Kash Official Kid Kash Official Kid Kash Official Kid Kash Official Kid Kash

Official Kid Kash Official Kid Kash Official Kid Kash Official Kid Kash Official Kid Kash Official Kid Kash

Official Kid Kash Official Kid Kash Official Kid Kash Official Kid Kash Official Kid Kash Official Kid Kash

Official Kid Kash Official Kid Kash Official Kid Kash Official Kid Kash Official Kid Kash Official Kid Kash

Official Kid Kash Official Kid Kash Official Kid Kash Official Kid Kash Official Kid Kash Official Kid Kash

Official Kid Kash Official Kid Kash Official Kid Kash Official Kid Kash Official Kid Kash Official Kid Kash

Official Kid Kash Official Kid Kash Official Kid Kash Official Kid Kash Official Kid Kash Official Kid Kash

Official Kid Kash Official Kid Kash Official Kid Kash Official Kid Kash Official Kid Kash Official Kid Kash

Official Kid Kash Official Kid Kash Official Kid Kash Official Kid Kash Official Kid Kash Official Kid Kash

Official Kid Kash Official Kid Kash Official Kid Kash Official Kid Kash Official Kid Kash Official Kid Kash

Official Kid Kash Official Kid Kash Official Kid Kash Official Kid Kash Official Kid Kash Official Kid Kash

Official Kid Kash Official Kid Kash Official Kid Kash Official Kid Kash Official Kid Kash Official Kid Kash

Official Kid Kash Official Kid Kash Official Kid Kash Official Kid Kash Official Kid Kash Official Kid Kash

Official Kid Kash Official Kid Kash Official Kid Kash Official Kid Kash Official Kid Kash Official Kid Kash

Official Kid Kash Official Kid Kash Official Kid Kash Official Kid Kash Official Kid Kash Official Kid Kash

Official Kid Kash Official Kid Kash Official Kid Kash Official Kid Kash Official Kid Kash Official Kid Kash

Official Kid Kash Official Kid Kash Official Kid Kash Official Kid Kash Official Kid Kash Official Kid Kash

The Kid Kash Program

Official Kid Kash Official Kid Kash Official Kid Kash Official Kid Kash Official Kid Kash Official Kid Kash

Official Kid Kash Official Kid Kash Official Kid Kash Official Kid Kash Official Kid Kash Official Kid Kash

Official Kid Kash Official Kid Kash Official Kid Kash Official Kid Kash Official Kid Kash Official Kid Kash

Official Kid Kash Official Kid Kash Official Kid Kash Official Kid Kash Official Kid Kash Official Kid Kash

Official Kid Kash Official Kid Kash Official Kid Kash Official Kid Kash Official Kid Kash Official Kid Kash

Official Kid Kash Official Kid Kash Official Kid Kash Official Kid Kash Official Kid Kash Official Kid Kash

Official Kid Kash Official Kid Kash Official Kid Kash Official Kid Kash Official Kid Kash Official Kid Kash

Official Kid Kash Official Kid Kash Official Kid Kash Official Kid Kash Official Kid Kash Official Kid Kash

Official Kid Kash Official Kid Kash Official Kid Kash Official Kid Kash Official Kid Kash Official Kid Kash

Official Kid Kash Official Kid Kash Official Kid Kash Official Kid Kash Official Kid Kash Official Kid Kash

Official Kid Kash Official Kid Kash Official Kid Kash Official Kid Kash Official Kid Kash Official Kid Kash

Official Kid Kash Official Kid Kash Official Kid Kash Official Kid Kash Official Kid Kash Official Kid Kash

Official Kid Kash Official Kid Kash Official Kid Kash Official Kid Kash Official Kid Kash Official Kid Kash

Official Kid Kash Official Kid Kash Official Kid Kash Official Kid Kash Official Kid Kash Official Kid Kash

Official Kid Kash Official Kid Kash Official Kid Kash Official Kid Kash Official Kid Kash Official Kid Kash

Official Kid Kash Official Kid Kash Official Kid Kash Official Kid Kash Official Kid Kash Official Kid Kash

Official Kid Kash Official Kid Kash Official Kid Kash Official Kid Kash Official Kid Kash Official Kid Kash

Official Kid Kash Official Kid Kash Official Kid Kash Official Kid Kash Official Kid Kash Official Kid Kash

Official Kid Kash Official Kid Kash Official Kid Kash Official Kid Kash Official Kid Kash Official Kid Kash

Official Kid Kash Official Kid Kash Official Kid Kash Official Kid Kash Official Kid Kash Official Kid Kash

Official Kid Kash Official Kid Kash Official Kid Kash Official Kid Kash Official Kid Kash Official Kid Kash

Official Kid Kash Official Kid Kash Official Kid Kash Official Kid Kash Official Kid Kash Official Kid Kash

Official Kid Kash Official Kid Kash Official Kid Kash Official Kid Kash Official Kid Kash Official Kid Kash

Official Kid Kash Official Kid Kash Official Kid Kash Official Kid Kash Official Kid Kash Official Kid Kash

Official Kid Kash Official Kid Kash Official Kid Kash Official Kid Kash Official Kid Kash Official Kid Kash

Official Kid Kash Official Kid Kash Official Kid Kash Official Kid Kash Official Kid Kash Official Kid Kash

The Kid Kash Program

Official Kid Kash Official Kid Kash Official Kid Kash Official Kid Kash Official Kid Kash Official Kid Kash
Official Kid Kash Official Kid Kash Official Kid Kash Official Kid Kash Official Kid Kash Official Kid Kash
Official Kid Kash Official Kid Kash Official Kid Kash Official Kid Kash Official Kid Kash Official Kid Kash
Official Kid Kash Official Kid Kash Official Kid Kash Official Kid Kash Official Kid Kash Official Kid Kash
Official Kid Kash Official Kid Kash Official Kid Kash Official Kid Kash Official Kid Kash Official Kid Kash
Official Kid Kash Official Kid Kash Official Kid Kash Official Kid Kash Official Kid Kash Official Kid Kash
Official Kid Kash Official Kid Kash Official Kid Kash Official Kid Kash Official Kid Kash Official Kid Kash
Official Kid Kash Official Kid Kash Official Kid Kash Official Kid Kash Official Kid Kash Official Kid Kash
Official Kid Kash Official Kid Kash Official Kid Kash Official Kid Kash Official Kid Kash Official Kid Kash
Official Kid Kash Official Kid Kash Official Kid Kash Official Kid Kash Official Kid Kash Official Kid Kash
Official Kid Kash Official Kid Kash Official Kid Kash Official Kid Kash Official Kid Kash Official Kid Kash
Official Kid Kash Official Kid Kash Official Kid Kash Official Kid Kash Official Kid Kash Official Kid Kash
Official Kid Kash Official Kid Kash Official Kid Kash Official Kid Kash Official Kid Kash Official Kid Kash
Official Kid Kash Official Kid Kash Official Kid Kash Official Kid Kash Official Kid Kash Official Kid Kash
Official Kid Kash Official Kid Kash Official Kid Kash Official Kid Kash Official Kid Kash Official Kid Kash
Official Kid Kash Official Kid Kash Official Kid Kash Official Kid Kash Official Kid Kash Official Kid Kash
Official Kid Kash Official Kid Kash Official Kid Kash Official Kid Kash Official Kid Kash Official Kid Kash
Official Kid Kash Official Kid Kash Official Kid Kash Official Kid Kash Official Kid Kash Official Kid Kash
Official Kid Kash Official Kid Kash Official Kid Kash Official Kid Kash Official Kid Kash Official Kid Kash
Official Kid Kash Official Kid Kash Official Kid Kash Official Kid Kash Official Kid Kash Official Kid Kash
Official Kid Kash Official Kid Kash Official Kid Kash Official Kid Kash Official Kid Kash Official Kid Kash
Official Kid Kash Official Kid Kash Official Kid Kash Official Kid Kash Official Kid Kash Official Kid Kash
Official Kid Kash Official Kid Kash Official Kid Kash Official Kid Kash Official Kid Kash Official Kid Kash
Official Kid Kash Official Kid Kash Official Kid Kash Official Kid Kash Official Kid Kash Official Kid Kash
Official Kid Kash Official Kid Kash Official Kid Kash Official Kid Kash Official Kid Kash Official Kid Kash
Official Kid Kash Official Kid Kash Official Kid Kash Official Kid Kash Official Kid Kash Official Kid Kash
Official Kid Kash Official Kid Kash Official Kid Kash Official Kid Kash Official Kid Kash Official Kid Kash

ISOLATION
BATHROOM PASS

ISOLATION
BATHROOM PASS

ISOLATION
BATHROOM PASS

© 2011 Rachel A. Wheeler

All rights reserved.

ISBN-10: 0615677126
ISBN-13: 978-0-615-67712-5

www.ingramcontent.com/pod-product-compliance
Lightning Source LLC
Chambersburg PA
CBHW061031180426
43194CB00037B/78